Contents

What Is a Plant?

Plants are all
around us.
They are living
things.
They come in all shapes
and sizes.

Plants All Around

WELDON OWEN PTY LTD
Publisher: Sheena Coupe
Senior Designer: Kylie Mulquin
Editorial Coordinators: Sarah Anderson,
Tracey Gibson
Production Manager: Helen Creeke
Production Assistant: Kylie Lawson

Project Editor: Ariana Klepac
Designer: Patricia Ansell
Text: Jan Stradling

05 04 03 02
10 9 8 7 6 5 4 3 2

Published in New Zealand by
Shortland Publications,
10 Cawley Street, Ellerslie, Auckland.
Published in the United Kingdom by
Kingscourt/McGraw-Hill,
Shoppenhangers Road, Maidenhead,
Berkshire, SL6 2QL.
Published in Australia by Mimosa Shortland,
8 Yarra Street, Hawthorn, Victoria 3122.

Printed in Singapore
ISBN: 0-7699-1242-7

CREDITS AND ACKNOWLEDGMENTS

PICTURE AND ILLUSTRATION CREDITS
[t=top, b=bottom, l=left, r=right, c=centre]
Ad-Libitum/S. Bowey 8b. 9c. Ray Grinaway 14tl. David Mackay 1c, 3tr, 6b, 10t,11br,11bl, 11tl, 11tr, 16b.
Iain McKellar 13br. Jane Pickering/Linden Artists 14c. Nicola Oram 4–5c. Photodisc 12b (Glen Allison), 13bl (Photolink).
PhotoEssentials banding. Barbara Rodanska 5r, 7c, 14r. Trevor Ruth 13tr. Chris Shorten 15.

Weldon Owen would like to thank the following people for their assistance in the production of this book:
Peta Gorman, Michael Hann, Marney Richardson.

Did You Know?

Seaweed is a plant. It lives in the sea.

Parts of a Plant

Plants have roots that hold them in place. Water travels from the roots up the stem. Leaves make food and flowers make seeds.

Flower

Leaf

Stem

Roots

7

How Do Plants Live?

Plants need energy from the Sun, the air and the soil to live. Plants use their leaves, roots and stems to take in food.

Try This

Put some celery into coloured water. Leave it overnight and see what happens.

The leaves take in carbon dioxide.

Flowers grow to make seeds for new plants.

The leaves send out oxygen.

The leaves take in energy from the Sun.

Food flows through the stems to other parts of the plant.

The roots take in food and water from the soil.

9

Pollen is used by some plants to make new plants.

Bees help carry pollen from flower to flower.

Pollen

New Life

Old plants make new plants in different ways. Some plants make seeds and others grow new plants from their roots or stems.

Daffodil bulbs
can grow
new bulbs.

Daffodil bulb

Strawberry

Strawberries
grow new plants
from their roots.

Pine cone

Seeds fall
to the ground
and grow
into new plants.

Dandelion

Where Plants Live

Some plants live in hot places and some plants live in cold places. Plants live almost everywhere.

Rainforest

Mountain

Grassland

Water

Desert

13

Clothes are made from cotton.

Foxgloves are used in medicine.

Nuts come from plants.

Useful Plants

We use plants every day. Plants give us materials for clothes, medicines and building. We also use plants as food.

Fruit and vegetables help keep us fit and healthy. We eat many parts of these plants.

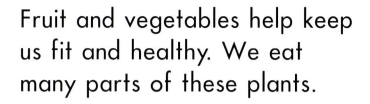

We eat the fruit of tomatoes.

We eat the roots of carrots.

We eat the leaves of lettuces.

Index